THE
NEW DAD
SURVIVAL HANDBOOK

Cheryl **Caldwell**

KPT PUBLISHING

So, you're a new DAD !

NOW WHAT?

For starters, don't expect love at first sight.
It could happen. Probably won't. It's normal.

DON'T WORRY

One day you'll be so in love with that little
flat-nosed-funny-looking-blotchy-skinned-
cone-headed baby, you won't know what
to do with yourself.

2

Congratulations!

You've fathered a new baby! That's right!

You're a

DAD!

You're not a backup parent. And don't let anyone, including yourself, tell you differently. You are a dad!

wHile
You're at the
HOSPITAL

You're going to be too tired, scared, excited, scared, confused, scared, and discombobulated to grasp much else at this point, so follow these instructions
(you'll look like a hero later, trust me)
(if you've already left the hospital, read this anyway, you may be able to salvage a few things - along with your hero status.)

4

- Buy a newspaper on the day your baby is born. If you forget, go down to the local newspaper office. They should have a few extras.

- Collect everyone's plastic ID bracelets, footprint certificate, hospital menu, etc...

- Jot down a few thoughts.

- Now put all of this stuff in a time capsule.

BOOM! HERO.

- Gather up as many of those little blankets (AKA swaddling cloths) as you can find. Sure, they'll give you one in the You're-Going-Home packet. Take more. You'll be glad you did. So will your wife.

The day before you come home, take several used* swaddling clothes and stash them around your house. Your dog can sniff them and get used to smelling your baby's scent in the (dog's) house before you even bring the baby home.

*This is important! Swaddling cloths MUST have been used by your baby! Unless, of course, you want your dog to accept someone else's baby or the launderer.

They've sent you home.

Seriously?

Yep.

NOW WHAT?

Basically, you're on your own.

SERIOUSLY?

YEP.

But I'm not ready, you say.
No one is, they answer.
Where's the instruction manual, you ask.
Like you've ever read the instructions,
everyone says (they are definitely thinking it).
Nevermind, I'll Google it, you say.
Remember when you Googled symptoms of the
common cold and thought you'd be dead by
morning? Same thing.

HINT: read this survival guide instead.

BREAST
YES ✓

For some new mothers breast feeding goes smoothly. Not always. For many it's hard and it hurts. Unless you're ready to give it a go, don't judge. Instead, when she's having trouble, do your best to transpose yourself into a zen rock of calm.

If she's able to breastfeed, once the baby is 3 mos old, encourage your wife to pump once a day so you can BOND and SHE CAN SLEEP.

FEEDING

You will be jealous of the time your baby spends with your wife's boobs (correction: her GIGANTIC boobs).

Zip it. Shut it.
Don't. Say. It.
I repeat, keep it to yourself.

She doesn't feel sexy, she feels like a machine. Try not to confuse the two. Instead, wait until later, then (say it with me) tell her she's beautiful. You can thank me later.

TOOLS:

A - a clean diaper (or six)

B - burping towel to lay over the front bits while you position the diaper or clean the back bits (particularly important if you are changing a baby boy).

C - baby wipes

D - diaper rash ointment, lotion, powder

E - toy or other distractor (will be needed more as your baby grows)

F - changing pad. You probably won't find a public restroom with a place to change your baby (particularly if you are flying solo). Bring a changing pad on all outings.

G - Hazmat Suit, respirator, and goggles are optional but recommended

H - change of clothes (for both baby and you)

Beyond the Diaper Change
AKA

THE

BLOW

OUT

Truth.
Some BLOW-OUTS can't be handled
outside of the tub.

Truth.
It WILL happen.

Truth.
It will be disgusting.

First,
see - Bathing Baby - on page 22

Second,
Go take a shower of your own.
You'll need it. Truth.

THE 3P MOMENT

THE FULL FATHER INITIATION

What is the 3P moment, you ask?
What is this Full Father Initiation of which you speak?
I'm glad you asked. Buckle up.

The 3P moment is the TRIFECTA,
that moment you are pee'd on,
pooped on, and puked on.

Three P's.
All at once.

Congratulations!

YOU'VE BEEN OFFICIALLY INITIATED INTO FATHERHOOD

19

A Word of Encouragement

Don't worry about being the perfect father.
You won't be. BUT. You'll be the perfect
father for your baby. You've got this.

BONUS:

Your wife will fall in love with you
all over again when she sees you being a daddy.

(which leads to another BONUS – see Question #1 page 44)

How to Bathe a Baby

#1 cut along dotted line

THIS END UP↑

#2 tape on baby's head

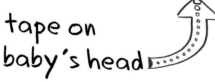

#3 Put baby in water
Warm - not hot (test with wrist)
2" deep - not 2 feet deep

BATH TIP OF THE DAY

Clean all of the creases and crevices.
ALL. OF. THEM.

between fingers
groin
elbows
neck

behind the knees
hiney
armpits
toes

HORRIBLE things hide in the creases.
Sidenote: There is no such thing as
using too many baby wipes. You're
welcome.

How to dress a baby:

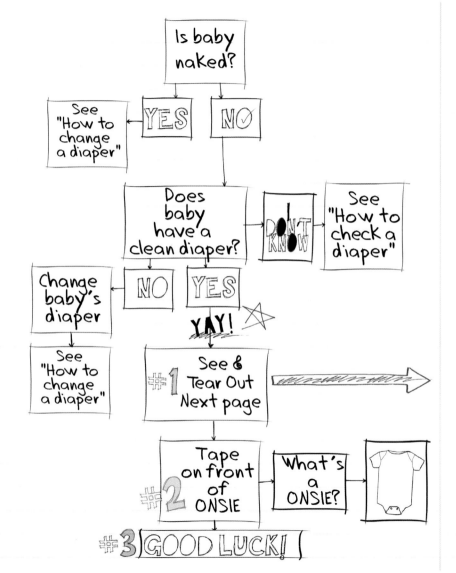

Baby Dressing Template:

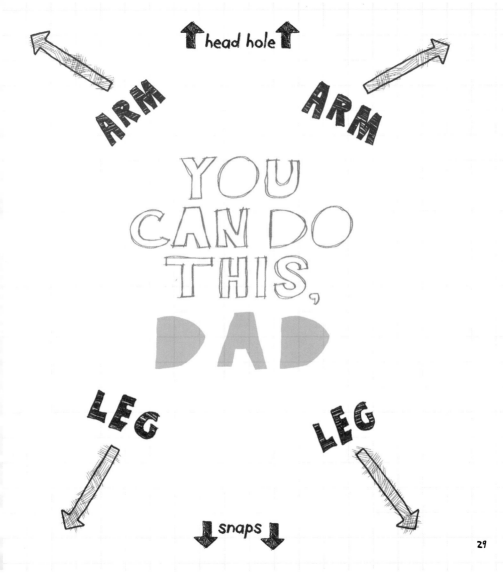

How tired will I be?

↓

this one is easy
ZOMBIE TIRED → How long will it last?

↓

I'd prefer not to answer that

↓

B - B - BUT...

↓

OK, OK. The first two months will be the hardest. → What happer after that?

You're gonna b a baby - feeding diaper - changi NINJA

↑

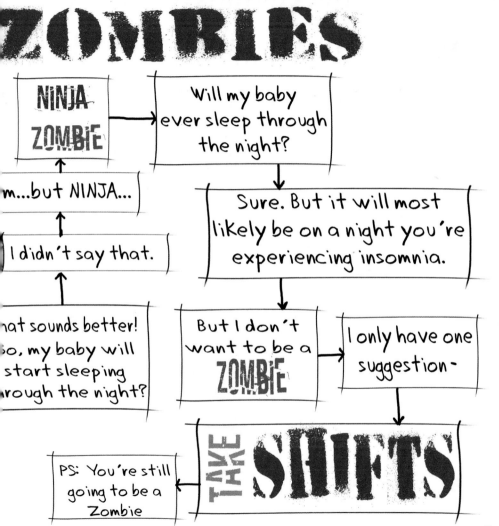

31

Fact #1:   Your baby will cry.

Fact #2:   It will make your skin crawl
             (partly with panic, partly
                     with sheer decibels)

Fact #3:   It will make your wife's skin
             crawl off.

Fact #4:   You won't always know why they
             are crying.
             Scenario #1
             Could be they are trying to
             communicate.

             Scenario #2
             Could be an explosion of pent up
             baby angst.

Fact #5:   At some point, you will probably
             cry too. It's ok. It's normal.

             No sleep = cry = normal.

How to PACIFY PENT UP baby ANGST

A) BOUNCE

No, not like you are on a 1950's pogo stick!

Instead, hold your baby to your chest and do deep knee bends.

34

) THE HANDOFF (Warning: You won't get any points for this one. Still...)

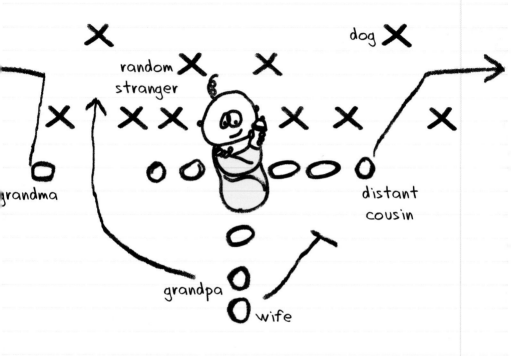

C) Still having a melt-down?
Don't waste anymore time guessing!
WALK OUTSIDE (bring baby with you)

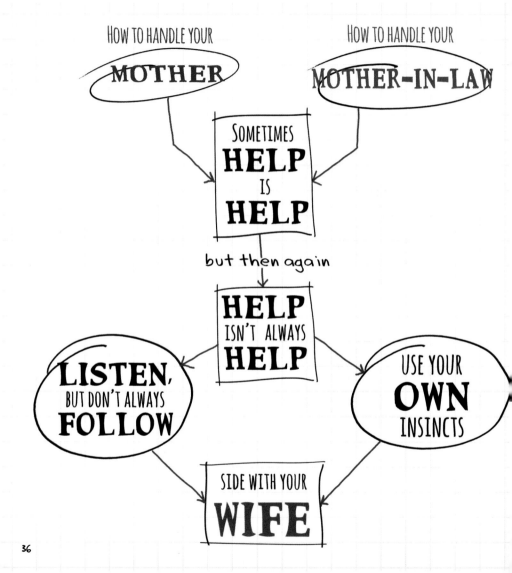

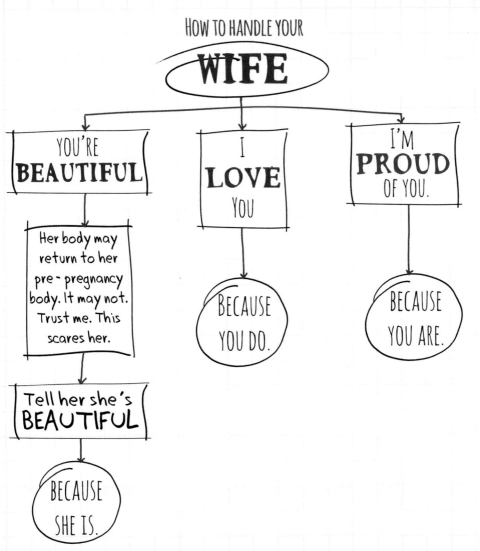

37

TRAVEL

Wait. We can travel?

ABSOLUTELY. In fact, the first three months may be the easiest. But since it takes about two months for you to figure out stuff (AKA turn into a **NINJA**) shoot for the third month.

It's easy to fall into the we-are-never-going-out-again-it's-easier-to-stay-at-home rut. Don't do it.

GO.

Get out into the world. You'll feel more normal. Plus, there will be perks - like popping straight to the front of the line. Take advantage of every perk you can.

TIP: Pack YOURSELF a few extra shirts. (see pic page 12)

You will be late for everything.

EVERYTHING.

'ry to leave 10 minutes earlier than you need to,
so you'll only be 10 minutes late.

THE BEST THING EVER

Your baby smiles.

Why do they smile, you ask?

HINT: fart

Still, it will melt your heart.

HELPING IS EASY

It ain't the 50's anymore. Plus, you're not a jerk.

＊throw a load of spit-up crusted clothes in the washer

＊make a bed

＊go grocery shopping, pick up take-out, or throw that lasagne your mother made into the oven

＊＊ Need encouragement? See Question #1 page 44

42

THINGS YOU CAN DO WITH YOUR BABY

RIGHT NOW

READ to your baby.

Take your baby **PLACES**

READ to your baby.

SING to your baby.

(No, they don't care if you can sing, or if you don't know any songs. Make one up. A bedtime - naptime one is great. They'll learn what to expect, like Pavlov's dogs.)

Have I mentioned **READ** to your baby?

A FEW QUESTIONS
YOU'VE BEEN WANTING TO ASK:

#1 Q) Am I still going to get laid?

A) Not for a few weeks. After that, yes. But not as much. There are some things that will increase your chances. You'll find them in this book.

#2 Q) Why is she crazy?

A) Hormones. (This is temporary.)

#3 Q) Why is her hair falling out and clogging the drain?

A) Also, hormones. Also, temporary. Stock up on Drano. You will need it around month 4.

#4 Q) Is there anything else I should know?

A) YES. Lots. Here's one. Your wife will still look pregnant after the baby is born.

Q) Wait. What? I knew it might take a while to lose the pregnancy weight, but I didn't know she'd still look pregnant!

A) She will. Your response? "You're beautiful and I love you."

Congratulations!

You now know what it's like to have your heart walk around outside of your body and be forevermore known as so-and-so's

Go on, pin this to your shirt.
You deserve it!

About the Author

Cheryl **Caldwell** is a sometimes artist, photographer, filmmaker, marine aquarist, and author. Most of her inspiration comes from her unconventional view of the world and the fact that she finds the mundane hilarious. She is owner of Co-edikit®, a humor based company that pairs comical illustrations with a witty combination of clear cut, down-to-earth words of wisdom and sarcastic humor. Her artwork and characters have been licensed and sold throughout the world. Her original paintings of the Co-edikit® characters can be found in several art galleries in the U.S., including Bee Galleries in New Orleans. She still subscribes to the philosophy that if you're having a bad day, ask a four- or five-year-old to skip. It's hysterical.

The New Dad Survival Handbook

Copyright © 2018 Cheryl Caldwell

Published by KPT Publishing
Minneapolis, Minnesota 55406
www.KPTPublishing.com

ISBN: 978-1-944833-41-1

Design and production by Koechel Peterson and Associates, Minneapolis, Minnesota

First printing May 2018

10 9 8 7 6 5 4 3 2

Printed in the United States of America